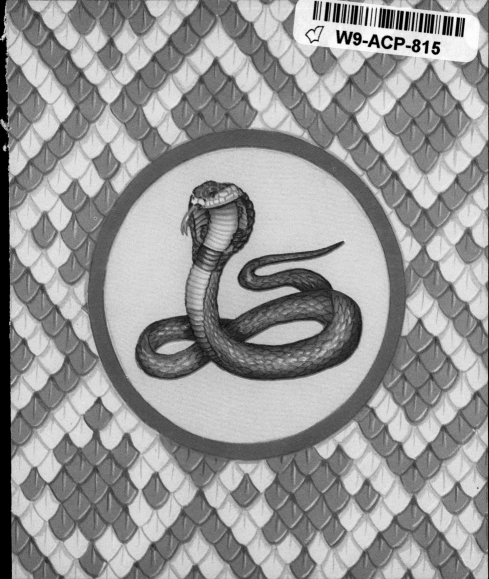

My Little Book of
SNAKES

By Gina Ingoglia
Illustrated by Rosiland Solomon

*John L. Behler, Curator, Department of Herpetology,
New York Zoological Society, Consultant*

A GOLDEN BOOK · NEW YORK
Western Publishing Company, Inc., Racine, Wisconsin 53404

What Are Snakes?

Snakes are graceful creatures that belong to a group of animals called reptiles, which means "crawlers."

Snakes can't hear. They can't close their eyes. The way that they smell is by waving their long, flickering tongues in the air.

Snakes live in almost every part of the world. Many live on the ground, but some live in trees. Still others spend most of their time in water.

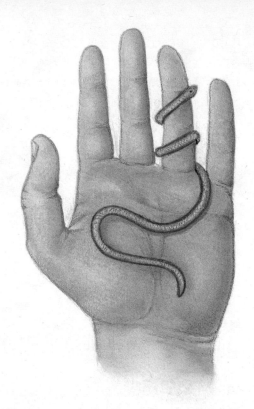

Little and Big

There are more than two thousand different kinds of snake. The thread snake is the smallest. It is only six inches long and not much thicker than a soda straw.

The python is the longest of all snakes. This giant grows to be thirty feet long—the length of a moving van!

The anaconda is the heaviest snake. Its body can be as big as the trunk of a large tree. It weighs as much as five hundred pounds or more. That's as much as a whole human family!

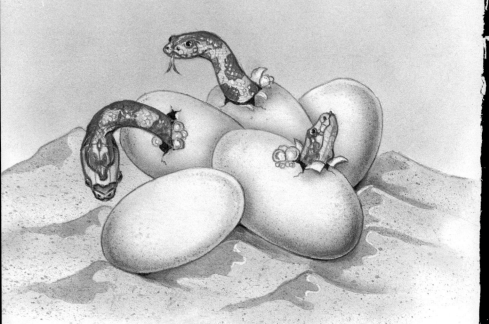

Baby Snakes

Most baby snakes hatch from leathery eggs. A baby corn snake has a tiny "egg tooth" that it uses to slit open its shell. The special tooth drops off in a few days.

A female earth snake does not lay eggs. Her babies grow inside her body and are born alive.

Moving Around

Like many snakes, the ribbon snake forms a long, wavy *S* as it travels across the ground. It pushes its body off stones and other objects to help it move forward.

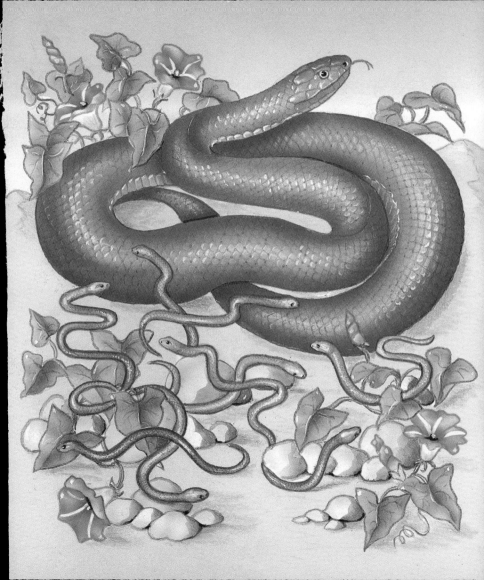

Moving Around

Like many snakes, the ribbon snake forms a long, wavy *S* as it travels across the ground. It pushes its body off stones and other objects to help it move forward.

Many snakes are good tree climbers. The black racer uses a spread-out "step-like" motion to hold on to rough spots in the bark.

A Brand-New Skin

Scales cover a snake's body. Several times a year, a snake grows a new skin under its worn and damaged old one.

This yellow rat snake crawls out of the neck of its old skin. It's like pulling off a long stocking.

Deadly Biters

Most snakes are not poisonous. However, the rattlesnake is one of a small group that *is* poisonous. A rattlesnake is named for the rattle on the end of its tail.

The rattlesnake has sharp hollow teeth called fangs. When a rattlesnake bites its prey, poison is squeezed out through the snake's fangs.

A poisonous cobra rises, flattening its neck into a wide hood. The cobra watches a snake charmer playing a flute. As the man sways from side to side, the cobra sways, too. But the cobra isn't swaying to the music. It's just keeping its eyes on the man moving in front of it.

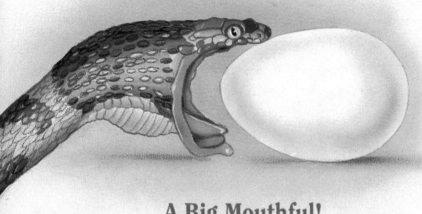

A Big Mouthful!

Snakes have special jaws that allow them to open their mouths much wider than humans can. A snake can swallow an object bigger than its head.

This African egg-eating snake stretches its jaws around a large egg. Inside the snake's neck, a sharp spine from the backbone breaks the egg shell. The inside of the egg empties into the snake's throat. Then the snake spits out the shell.

A Long Nap

Snakes spend cold winters in a kind of sleep called *hibernation*.

Tangled together, hundreds of garter snakes may hibernate together in an underground den. In the spring, the snakes crawl out of their den. They warm up slowly in the sun and then crawl away.

Hidden From View

The color and shape of a snake's body often help it to survive. The green mamba lives in trees. Its long, slim green body blends in perfectly with the leaves and twisted vines. It can sneak up on its prey or hide from its enemies unseen.

The markings on the body of a copperhead snake match the dead dry leaves on the ground. The snake can hide very well in these leaves.

Champion Swimmers

Sea snakes live in the ocean. They have flat tails that they use like paddles to push themselves quickly through the salt water. Like all snakes, sea snakes have lungs and must come to the water's surface to breathe. But they can stay underwater for a very long time—eight hours on one breath!

Made for "Flying"

The slender paradise tree snake is quite at home in jungle treetops. When surprised by an enemy, it rushes to the end of a branch and leaps into the air. It spreads its ribs and flattens its body and glides to safety in a nearby tree.

Playing Tricks

Some snakes have developed special ways of protecting themselves. To scare its enemies, the gentle hog-nosed snake swells up and hisses wildly.

If this doesn't work, the snake rolls over and plays dead. If the snake is turned rightside up, it flips itself over again—as if to prove it's really dead!

Sharing the World

Some people are afraid of snakes. They think all snakes are dangerous and often try to kill them. But every animal on earth has a right to live, including the snake.

If you are lucky enough to see a snake resting on a rock or hurrying off someplace, don't bother it. A snake is a wild animal and should be left alone, free to live its life in the world of nature.